**Two cats
groom the
ski hill just
for you**

2

Doubl... Diamond Run, Nakiska

3

Three bears slide down mountain scree

Rocky Mountain
123s

Jocey Asnong

RMB

Mount Rundle

1

One new cub is ready for fun!

4

Four foxes fix their eyes on the waterfalls

Takakkaw Falls

Five ravens learn to skydive

5

6

Six lynx practise snowboard tricks

Seven bikers race to the bottom

Mount Seven, Golden

7

8

Eight elk try to skate

Lake Louise, Alberta

Nine goats
climb a hard line

Maligne Canyon

9

10

**Ten peaks tower
above our den**

Eleven moose are
loose in the fen

Mount Engadine, Kananaskis

11

**Twelve tents
light up the night**

12

Mount Robson

13

**Thirteen climbers
that we can see**

14

Fourteen skiers fly down a steep slope

Fernie

Lake O'Hara

**Fifteen footprints
are made in the snow**

15

Sixteen mittens dry
above our warm fire

Storm Mountain

16

Bow River

17

**Seventeen fish
swim below
our canoe**

18

Eighteen
ears hear a
midnight
howl

Jasper National Park

19

**Nineteen
snowflakes fall
from the sky**

20

Larch Valley

Twenty marmots at our picnic are just too many!

JOCEY ASNONG was raised by a pack of wild pencil crayons in a house made out of paper and stories. When she is not chasing her cats around her art cave in Canmore, Alberta, she might be caught in a blizzard near Mount Everest, or running away from wolf dogs in Mongolia, or peeking out castle windows in Scotland, or sleeping under the stars in Bolivia. Jocey's books for children include *Nuptse and Lhotse Go to the Rockies* (RMB, 2014), *Nuptse and Lhotse Go to Iceland* (RMB, 2015), *Rocky Mountain ABCs* (RMB, 2016) and *Rocky Mountain 123s* (RMB, 2017).

1 2 3 4 5 6 7

8 9 10 11 12

13 14 15 16

17 18 19 20

RMB | Rocky Mountain Books Ltd.
rmbooks.com
@rmbooks
facebook.com/rmbooks

Cataloguing data available from Library and Archives Canada
ISBN 978-1-77160-211-2 (board book)
ISBN 978-1-77160-501-4 (softcover)
ISBN 978-1-77160-502-1 (electronic)

Design by Chyla Cardinal

Printed and bound in China

Distributed in Canada by Heritage Group Distribution and in the U.S. by Publishers Group West

For information on purchasing bulk quantities of this book, or to obtain media excerpts or invite the author to speak at an event, please visit rmbooks.com and select the "Contact Us" tab.

RMB | Rocky Mountain Books is dedicated to the environment and committed to reducing the destruction of old-growth forests. Our books are produced with respect for the future and consideration for the past.

We acknowledge the financial support of the Government of Canada through the Canada Book Fund and the Canada Council for the Arts, and of the province of British Columbia through the British Columbia Arts Council and the Book Publishing Tax Credit.

Canada Council
for the Arts
Conseil des arts
du Canada